A Mississippi *Summer* on Bluebird Hill

A true story about our little farm in the hills of Southern Mississippi

Printed in the United States of America.

ISBN: 1-59571-073-6
Library of Congress Control Number: 2005925722

Hot Chocolate Books
a division of Word Association Publishers
205 Fifth Avenue,
Tarentum, Pennsylvania 15084
www.wordassociation.com

A Mississippi *SUMMER* on Bluebird Hill

A true story about our little
farm in the hills of Southern Mississippi

by
Billie Remson

Hot Chocolate BOOKS

A Division of

Word Association Publishers
205 Fifth Avenue
Tarentum, Pennsylvania 15084

Written for children and adults who would like to know
what life is like living on a farm for the fun of it.
And for those who just enjoy remembering

Dedicated to my grandchildren who bring a smile
to my face and happiness to my life.

I love you, Mama B

SUMMER

The little farm of Bluebird Hill is especially beautiful in late June, with the hot summer sun smiling down and the large, sweet-smelling magnolia flowers showing off their big, show-off blooms. They are so beautiful against the dark green shiny evergreen leaves. No wonder the magnolia is Mississippi's state tree and its flower, the state flower. If you come to Mississippi and you enter along one of the major highways, you'll be greeted by an avenue of beautiful magnolia trees planted there just to welcome visitors.

Mama B has been picking blueberries in the orchard. It takes Mama B awhile to pick a bucketful of the delicious berries because she eats more than she puts in the bucket. She

stands up straight now to stretch her back and with her hands on her hips, she takes a deep breath. *Mmmmm, ahhhhh*, she smells the woodsy fragrance of pine blowing in the warm breeze.

On the way back to the house she meets up with Papa Doc, who has been doing some work on his tractor, after a long morning of mowing. The two walk past the picket fence surrounding the flower garden. They stop for a moment to admire the roses. Southern Mississippi's hot summer days and afternoon thunderstorms produce many colorful flowers. The watermelon-red flowers of the crepe myrtle trees are in full bloom at the edge of the flower garden. What a summer show Mississippi puts on!

Mama B and Papa Doc stand very still and watch the butterflies with their bright colors as they

fly in circles, trying to decide what flower to land on. They are gathering nectar to fuel their energetic bodies.

"They seem to like our butterfly bush best of all," says Mama B.

"What's that I hear in the grass, Mama B?"

Papa Doc points in the direction of a turtle making its way down the hill to the pond. The turtle is looking for water. It will be surprised to find several other turtles are already at the pond. One group of turtles is lined up on a log facing the same direction enjoying the warm morning sun on their thick hard shells. Slowly but surely the turtle in the yard, with his neck stretched as high as possible, makes his way down the hill to the pond.

As they watch the turtle crawling first one

way then the other, down the hill, a twig hits Papa Doc on top of his head. He looks up and sees Fritz, the unusual squirrel with the unusual name, high up in the big old oak tree, wanting attention. Fritz is putting on a little show, jumping from limb to limb, like an acrobat almost missing a limb on purpose and catching on with his sharp finger nails. He dangles for a few seconds then pulls himself up on the limb and sits with his front feet under his chin, while flicking his tail at Mama B and Papa Doc.

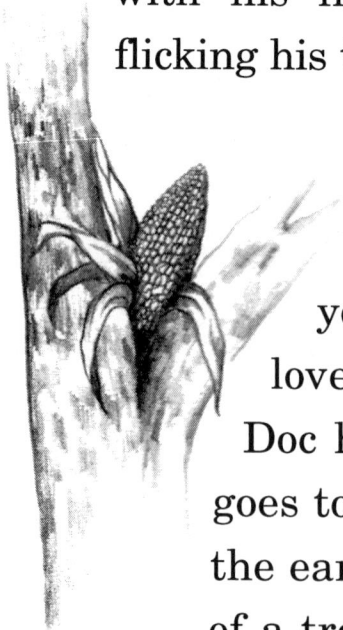

"Why Fritz," Mama B says, "that was such a nice show. I am going to the barn and get you an ear of corn." Mama B just loves to spoil Fritz. She hands Papa Doc her bucket of berries and off she goes to the barn. Mama B returns with the ear of corn and places it in the fork of a tree limb in the big oak tree. The corn is a treat for the daring show put on by their unusual squirrel with the unusual name who lives in the big oak tree and calls Bluebird Hill home.

School vacation has started. Alex and Austin will soon arrive on Bluebird Hill to spend a little time on the farm with their grandparents, Mama B and Papa Doc. One of their favorite things to do at the farm is fish in the pond. Papa Doc has put up an automatic fish feeder that feeds the fish twice a day. The boys will enjoy watching the fish come to the top of the water with a splash to eat the granules of food floating on the water.

Papa Doc and Mama B have been working hard for the past two days. They are trying to get the large yard looking picture-perfect before the arrival of the grandchildren on Bluebird Hill. Mama B mows the grass with the riding lawn mower in the cool of the early morning. Papa Doc, who also favors the morning, mows with the finishing mower attached to the tractor. But just as they finish, it's time to start again and on and on it goes.

Time for an ice cold glass of lemonade on the back porch. As they rest, they watch four birds splash in the cool water of the birdbath. As the birds come out of the water, they perch on a limb over the birdbath and shake the excess water from their feathers. They use their beaks to oil and fluff their feathers and with a good shake, all their feathers fall into place. Fritz has come down the old oak tree and picked up the ear of corn Mama B left for him. He is holding the corn with his hands and using his tail to balance as he eats the dry corn from the cob.

Bo is standing on the edge of the porch watching Fritz and the birds. His tail is high in the air and he is wagging it back and forth while making a whining sound. Mama B knows he is ready to lunge off the porch and chase the birds and Fritz away. *Bark! Bark! Bark!*

"NOOOOOO, Bo, NO!" she commands. Bo

obediently lowers his tail, looks at Mama B and lies down on the edge of the porch with his head resting between his paws. Oh, he'll stay put and stop his barking but he can't help rolling his big brown eyes back and forth as he watches the birds and Fritz. He realizes this fun-time has come to an end before it ever got started, thanks to Mama B.

Papa Doc has finished drinking his lemonade. He takes off his cap, wipes his forehead, and takes a deep breath.

"Mama B," he says, "there must be an easier way to keep this grass mowed. This is a fulltime job for both of us in the hot summertime. I have been so busy with mowing the grass I have not had time to work in my vegetable garden. And I know you've had to put off a hundred things you'd like to be doing. There doesn't seem to be time for anything but mowing, mowing, and more mowing!"

During the winter, Mama B and Papa Doc spent many long, winter evenings planning summertime trips. One favorite was a drive down to Gulfport, Mississippi to relax on the beautiful white sand beaches of Mississippi's Gulf coast. The also talked about taking a pleasant, little jaunt along what they call the circle, which is a fifty-mile drive from Tylertown, where

Bluebird Hill is, over to the
little towns of Collins,

Seminary, and on into bustling Hattiesburg.
They have many friends and many lovely sites to
enjoy along the way. They are anxious to take a
hike on Longleaf Trace and maybe even invite
some of the grandchildren to join them. The
young ones might like bringing their bikes and
riding the distance.

Longleaf is a forty-one mile hiking, biking, and horse-riding trail that begins in Hattiesburg, Mississippi and goes all the way to Prentiss. Papa Doc loves this trail because it's so beautifully shaded. Mama B appreciates it because it's nearly all level land. It was once a great rail line. Both Mama B and Papa Doc like to tell their grandchildren stories about the trains that used to carry passengers and freight along that line. But truly, with all the mowing, they haven't had a moment to think about any such outings.

Mama B has been waiting for the opportunity to talk to Papa Doc. She has a solution to the mowing problem—it's cows! And this is the perfect time to make her case.

Now, to be honest, the cow suggestion is not just about the mowing. The truth is Mama B would dearly love to have a baby calf born on Bluebird Hill because, well, she loves baby calves. And the only way to have a baby calf is to buy cows to be the Mamas and a bull, who will be the Daddy. But if she simply told Papa Doc she would like to have a baby calf on the farm, he might think she was just adding to all the work. After all, Papa Doc didn't grow up on a farm like Mama B did. He doesn't always know the ins and outs of farm life.

As much as Mama B and Papa Doc both love Bluebird Hill, they also like to have fun traveling around this beautiful part of Mississippi. To make matters worse, they hardly have enough time to do their *most* favorite thing—sitting on the farmhouse porch enjoying the view.

"Every farm needs cows," Mama B finally announces. And before Papa Doc can say 'but cows mean more work,' she quickly adds, "cows like to eat grass, lots and lots of grass, more grass than we can mow in a whole day!"

Now she has Papa Doc's attention. His little brown beaded eyes begin to twinkle.

Mama B is very encouraged and she goes on. "How about we fence in part of the yard and the valley in front of the farmhouse. This will create a great pasture for a few cows and the pond will be a wonderful source of water for them."

Mama B can tell that Papa Doc is liking what he hears. He is so tired of mowing the grass.

"And," says Mama B who just won't rest unless she comes clean, "to be perfectly honest, I would dearly love having a newborn, baby calf on Bluebird Hill."

As always, Papa Doc wants to please Mama B. Once Papa Doc decides on a project, there is no stopping him. The very next day he goes to Tylertown Farm Supply and buys the supplies he needs to start a fence project. In no time at all, he is busy planning the outline of a barbed wire fence around the grassy pasture, including part of the yard. A barb is a small piece of sharp wire, attached to wire, about eight inches apart.

The barb will stick the cows if they push on the fence. Cows will push on a fence trying to eat the grass just outside the fence. As the saying goes, grass is always greener on the other side of the fence, or so it seems.

Papa Doc has hired a fence builder to help him place the fence posts around the pasture and attach the barb wire to the posts. Gates are added for easy access to the pasture. When they finish building the fence Papa Doc goes back to Tylertown Farm Supply where he buys a salt block that contains vitamins and minerals. He also buys a tub of protein for the cows to lick and a fifty pound bag of sweet feed, as a treat for the cows. All of these goodies and the lush green grass in the pasture will create a happy home for the new arrivals.

"All we need now are cows", Mama B tells Papa Doc late Monday afternoon.

"What do you say we go into town early tomorrow morning for the weekly livestock auction. We'll surely find some fine cows there," Papa Doc answers.

Mama B and Papa Doc get up early the next morning, anxious to go to the auction and buy their cows. They have asked a friend who knows all about buying cows to join them. The three arrive two hours early and climb the steps to the raised platform of the outside holding pen. Standing on the platform, they get a bird's-eye view of all the animals in the holding pen below. As the animals are unloaded from the farmers' trailers, Papa Doc and Mama B see if they can spot the perfect cows for Bluebird Hill. There are several hundred cattle brought to the auction by other farmers to sell.

Farmers have plenty of green grass in their pastures in the spring and summer. So the grazing is good. The farmers are taking advantage of their nice, fat cattle bringing a good selling price. Cattle usually means a mixture of cows, bulls, heifers and calves. A cow is a female and a bull is a male. A group of cattle is a herd. A calf is a young cow or bull. The selling price of a cow is determined by how much a cow weighs and the overall condition of the cow. Cows can weigh from 900 to 2,000 pounds. Bulls may weigh 2,000 pounds or more.

The cows are brought into the auction sale ring, usually in groups of one to six at a time. The auctioneer begins the bidding. Everyone takes a seat just outside the sale ring. Mama B and Papa Doc understand very few words the auctioneer is saying. He is talking very, very fast and using words they never heard before. Their friend will be doing the bidding for them. He understands the fast talking language of the auctioneer.

The choice is hard for Mama B and Papa Doc but finally they spot the perfect cows, a big red one, a lovely black and white and her beautiful black calf. Their friend agrees that they have made good choices. The bidding goes well and soon Mama B and Papa Doc are the

proud owners of two cows and a calf. Now they head back to Bluebird Hill to prepare for the delivery of their new additions.

It is July and the burning afternoon sun is just beginning to set in the west when Bo's bark notifies Mama B and Papa Doc that someone is coming down the gravel road to Bluebird Hill. They hear the roar of a truck and the rattle of the trailer loaded with the big red cow and the black and white cow and her calf. The trailer makes a lot of noise as it is being pulled down the gravel road by the big truck. The hot, dusty cows are looking between the side rails of the trailer. Mama B and Papa Doc hope the cows like what they see of their new home on Bluebird Hill. Bo runs ahead of the truck, barking and wagging his white-tipped tail. He leads the way down the hill to the pasture gate.

The driver of the truck backs the trailer up to the pasture gate and opens the back gate of the trailer. Papa Doc opens the gate to the pasture and the cows run out of the trailer like a stampede. They clearly didn't care for the trailer. They run as fast as they can until they reach the back of the pasture where they feel safe.

The cows spend time by themselves getting to know their new surroundings. They graze the lush green grass by moving their heads back and forth along the grass. They cannot bite off grass because they do not have cutting teeth in the front of their upper jaw. They tear the grass by moving their head. Adult cattle have thirty-two teeth. They have eight teeth in the front of the lower jaw and twelve each in the back of the upper and lower jaws. As they graze and walk they discover the pond filled with fresh water. When they see the big pond they run to the water's edge. It has been a long hot day for the cows. The many summer storms have filled the pond so the water is deep and cool. The poor cows have not had water to drink all day and they are very thirsty. They stop at the edge of the pond for their first drink of water. How good that water must taste. Then all three move knee-deep into the water. The cool water tastes so good and feels so good to their legs as they stand in the shallow water to drink. They slowly wade out into the pond and they continue to drink and cool their hot bodies. They drink and wade, drink and wade until all that can be seen are their heads and a little part of their backs sticking out of the water. They are cool at last. Surely they like their new home on Bluebird Hill.

The noise of the cows startles a group of turtles that are sunning on a log. Several

splashes are heard as, one after the other, the turtles jump into the water. The turtles immediately swim to the automatic fish feeder that has just sprinkled fish food in the water. As the granules of food float on top of the water the turtles leave little for the fish.

The next morning Papa Doc is at the fence with a bucket of sweet feed for the cows. He calls the cows with his special call of "Whoooooooo cows, Whooooooo cows." The cows begin lowing, another word for mooing, and come running to the fence. They have heard this call, or one similar, before. While they are eating their feed from the bucket in Papa Doc's hand, one at a time, they are busy swishing their tails. Their long tail has thick bushy hair at the end. They swish their tails over their back to shoo-away the insects that bite them.

Papa Doc looks over his new herd and

notices the black and white cow is a little thin but realizes she has a calf that she is still nursing. That probably accounts for her size. The big red cow is much larger than the black and white, but she does not have a calf to nurse. She is in excellent condition, just large in size and a little slow in getting around. She is always grazing and makes her way slowly to the fence when Papa Doc arrives with a treat in his hand.

Bo is happy with his new friends. Shetland Sheepdogs were developed in the Shetland Islands of Scotland to herd sheep. Bo's natural instinct of herding tells him fun days are ahead. He lies down on the grass in the pasture in front of the cows and they come to him. He runs around the cows in circles, playing a game. When the cows get tired of Bo they chase him out of the pasture. Then he runs back to the farm house to wait on the porch for Papa Doc.

Today is an exciting day on Bluebird Hill.

This is the day Mama B and Papa Doc have been looking forward to for months. Their grandsons, Alex and Austin are arriving for a whole week's vacation. Papa Doc and Mama B have been discussing what they will do to entertain the children when they arrive on the farm.

Papa Doc has spotted a large wasps' nest on the barn that is full of larvae. Larvae are the little white cocoons in the wasps' nest that will hatch into wasps. The larvae from a wasp's nest are excellent fish bait, especially if you are trying to catch bream. The children will enjoy catching the small bream in the pond using the larvae as fish bait. Mama B fries the little fish as crisp as a potato chips *mmmm sooo good!* She amazes Papa Doc because there are very few fish bones on her plate when she finishes eating bream. The children may not eat the bream but Mama B will certainly enjoy their catch of the day.

Bluebird Hill is alive now with shouts and giggles. Alex is pushing Austin as high as he possibly can on the tire swing hanging from the old oak tree. Alex is running under the swing as he pushes Austin with his arms extended high over his head. As Alex lets go of the swing, Austin squeals and begs to go even higher. The little boys are cousins and live in different states. They have not seen each other since Christmas and had just about forgotten how much fun the farm can be especially when you get to share the fun with your cousin.

Papa Doc calls the boys over to the picnic table to rest and discuss their plans for their first fishing trip, down the hill to the pond.

Out the door comes Mama B with a tray of Kool Aid and cookies. Picky eater, Austin, wants to know what kind of cookies they are and Mama B tells him they are called hay stacks.   Both boys start giggling and joking with each other about eating cow food. And eat they do!   But the cousins soon snap to attention when Papa Doc announces that he has the small boat ready at the edge of the pond with paddles and life jackets. He has the large wasp's nest for bait and has new fishing lines on cane poles. During this first fishing discussion Papa Doc tells the boys that Austin will be the chief paddler. Since Alex is older and taller than Austin, he will be the lookout, on alert for waves or any indication that a fish or turtle is nearby. Alex and Austin can hardly wait for tomorrow and their first day of fishing.

It's early morning as Mama B prepares a

good country breakfast of fresh eggs, bacon, and hot biscuits. Alex enjoys it thoroughly, but Austin only wants a buttered biscuit and a glass of milk. Papa Doc has his usual cereal. Once they finish, Papa Doc and the boys head down the hill to the pond. Standing by the boat, putting on their life jackets, the three have a lengthy discussion about who is going to sit where. Once it's settled, they carefully board the little flat boat—ready to fish.

Chief paddler, Austin splashes wildly to get them into deeper water. Alex and Papa Doc don't mind getting a little wet on this warm summer morning. They know that Austin is taking his job seriously and doing his very best. In time, the boat and three fishermen arrive at the center of the pond. After a while, the waves settle and serious fishing begins. The boys quickly learn that the tender larvae of the wasps' nest are a favorite food of both the bream *and* turtles. The problem is that the turtles are eating the bait so quickly that most the bream can't get to it.

"We have to do something about these turtles." Papa Doc says. "Do either of you boys have any ideas?"

No answer from the boys.

"Alright, how about this," says Papa Doc. "I have a crab trap. Let's bait it with the heads from the bream we've caught and see if the turtles will go into the trap tonight."

The boys think this is a great idea. Once they are back on shore, they help Papa Doc clean the fish and prepare the turtle bait. From the front porch Mama B calls to Papa Doc and the boys "Ya'll come and eat, it's supper time!" Austin, the picky eater asks, "What are we having?" Mama B, laughing and teasing Austin says, "A thousand and one things."

Austin looks at Mama B with a curious expression as Mama B continues, "A thousand peas and one piece of cornbread." Then after a short pause, Mama B adds, "But for you, Austin it's chicken tenders and macaroni and cheese."

Kym Garraway...

Kym Garraway

Kym Garraway

After supper, Papa Doc and the boys bait the crab trap and place it in the shallow water of the pond. The next morning the boys are eager to go back to the pond and check their new turtle trap. Yes, it worked! The turtles are swimming around in the trap. The boys are thrilled. Now, they load the trap into the back of the pickup truck. Papa Doc and the boys take the trap to a creek about two miles from the farm and release the turtles in the cool running water. The turtles will have plenty of logs to rest on and good food to eat as they drift slowly down the cool water of the winding creek *away* from Bluebird Hill.

The week passes so quickly. The boys are having great fun on Bluebird Hill. When their parents arrive to pick them up, all they talk about is trapping and relocating the turtles. Papa Doc is pleased that he has found a new way to trap turtles and entertain the boys.

It's an especially hot, buggy, muggy, Mississippi summer afternoon. There is almost no breeze. Mama B and Papa Doc are sitting on the front porch drinking ice water.

"The vegetable garden and pretty summer flowers are beginning to wilt," says Mama B as she reaches for her watermelon-shaped fan to cool her face.

"Look at those big, gray cumulus clouds over there, Mama B. I think we're in for a good old thunderstorm."

Bo, who had been busy sniffing a mouse hiding in the wood that's stacked neatly on the porch, comes right over to Mama B. It seems the mere mention of a storm has caught his attention. Bo is not a happy dog when thunder rolls across his patch of Mississippi sky.

The wind picks up and a few sprigs of mistletoe from the old oak tree scatter across the yard. The smell of rain is in the air. Mama B jumps as a loud boom of thunder rolls across the heavens. The thunder alerts the animals of

Bluebird Hill that danger is approaching. Instinct tells them to take cover for protection. The cows had been in the pond cooling their bodies from the afternoon heat. Now they are heading up the hill to the pine tree thicket where they will take shelter. The chickens continue to scratch and peck in the chicken yard until rain begins to pelt their feathers. They make their way into the chicken house where raindrops are beating out a loud pitter-patter on the tin roof. Always cautious, Mama B takes Bo inside— like Bo, Mama B gets a little nervous during a thunderstorm.

Papa Doc, on the other hand, enjoys nature and her dramatic displays. He likes nothing better than listening to the symphony of the roaring wind and the rain's rat-a-tat-tat while counting the seconds between thunder booms to determine how far the storm is from Bluebird Hill. He smiles as he watches the big, fat drops dance on the water in the pond as the wind whips up frothy, little, white waves.

"Oh, this is pretty, Mama B," he calls through the screen door, into the house.

But Mama B has her hands full with Bo. She sits on a pillow on the floor scratching Bo's tummy to help him keep his mind off the storm. And, of course her comforting Bo, helps to keep her mind off the storm. So they help each other.

Boom! Thunder jars the windows of the little farmhouse. Bo is up in a flash with his paws on the window sill, *Bark! Bark! Bark!* As if he can scare the storm away. Perhaps he does. Just like that, the storm passes and Mama B and Bo venture back out onto the porch where Papa Doc is waiting. The dripping flowers are perking their little heads up and the chickens are happily pecking the wet dirt in the chicken

yard. But it's the birds who are really celebrating the rain shower—they are flying an aerial ballet in the brightening sky.

The air is fresh and fragrant and a cool breeze is rocking the pine trees.

Almost since their arrival on Bluebird Hill, Papa Doc has made a habit of feeding the cows sweet feed every morning as a little treat. They stand at the fence and wait for Papa Doc to come from the barn with the small white bucket of sweet feed swinging in his hand.

Although Mama B and Papa Doc have named the cows, cows don't respond to names. Cattle are not as intelligent as dogs. They respond as a group. Here they come, running up the fence line as Papa Doc calls "Whoooooooo Cows, Whoooooooo Cows!"

Curiously, the big red cow, now named Cayenne because of her deep red color, has been showing less and less interest in Papa Doc's call.

Today, when Papa Doc arrives, only Mower (named for her great talent of keeping the grass trimmed) and her calf, Midnight, come to the fence. Papa Doc doesn't know very much about cows, but he knows enough to be worried about Cayenne.

That evening, sitting on the porch, Papa Doc decides to wait one more day before telling Mama B about Cayenne's behavior. Mama B has been so excited about the cows that he doesn't want to do anything to disturb her happiness.

The next day, Cayenne is nowhere to be seen. The Mower is already waiting patiently by the fence. Young Midnight comes running up the hill with her tail almost straight out when she sees the bucket in Papa Doc's hand. Her body is rocking like a rocking chair, back and forth, as she runs as fast as her four hoofs will carry her. She is ready for her treat. She moos softly and is probably saying in cow language, *move over Mama Mower, I want some!*

After feeding the Mower and Midnight,

Papa Doc hurries down to the back of the pasture looking for Cayenne. He is very worried about her. *Oh, where can that cow be!* He thinks.

Papa Doc looks here and there, near and far but there is no sight of Cayenne. *What could have happened to her?*

Then, at last, just at the edge of the woods, he sees her. And when he realizes what he is seeing, he has to blink his little brown beaded eyes and look again and again. The big red cow, their Cayenne, has given Mama B what she has been wanting on Bluebird Hill, a beautiful, baby calf! The calf has just been born and is stumbling around trying to stand up and walk. As it tries to stand, its knees bend and it wobbles around in a most adorable way.

Papa Doc can't get up to the farmhouse fast enough.

"Mama B! Mama B! Come quickly and see what we have!"

In a flash Mama B is outside running toward Papa Doc.

"What is the matter?"

"Come with me to the pasture. Cayenne, the big, red....oh, you have to see for yourself!"

When Mama B and Papa Doc reach the back of the pasture, Cayenne is busy licking her baby calf to show her motherly love. Papa Doc and Mama B keep a safe distance because they know animals are very protective of their babies.

But Mama B can hardly contain her happiness.

"Oh what a beautiful calf! What a surprise this wonderful cow has given us! Bluebird Hill has a newborn calf!" And Mama B and Papa Doc just stand there and watch the cow and her calf with great joy and pride.

On that very day, on that very spot, Mama B and Papa Doc decide to give the big red cow a new name. She is no longer Cayenne—she is officially Mama Cow.

Mama Cow walks and the baby calf follows to a place in tall grass where the baby calf lays down. This is Mama Cow's way of hiding the calf to keep it safe from a coyote or other animals that may harm the new creature. Mama Cow moves away from her sleeping baby to graze the grass nearby. But she will keep a close watch to be sure her little one is safe.

A few days later Mama Cow is at the fence with the Mower, and Midnight for her treat of sweet feed. The dark red baby calf is standing right by her side sucking milk from the cow's udder, which is the bag that holds a cow's milk. The baby calf is getting so much milk that bubbles are coming out of its mouth. Mama B tells Papa Doc the deep red color of the baby calf is the color of paprika, a spice used for cooking. Papa Doc says, "Well, since she is a heifer, let's name her Paprika." Paprika is a great surprise addition to the Bluebird Hill farm family.

"We got two for the price of one." says Papa Doc.

Bo and Paprika make friends immediately. They are about the same size. Mama Cow watches as Bo and Paprika play and run around each other, stopping long enough to touch noses to seal their friendship.

"With two cows and two heifers, that will

grow up to be cows, we need to buy a bull so we can continue having baby calves," Mama B explains to Papa Doc.

Papa Doc is so happy with the whole cow venture that he is more than ready for this next step. "Our neighbor, Mr. Kahoe, has a young bull for sale. I'll go and talk to him." The next day Papa Doc goes to Mr. Kahoe's farm and buys his six month old, five hundred pound, Black Angus bull. The young bull is black all over his body.

When he is grown, he will be a handsome mate
for the cows of Bluebird Hill. "Let's name him
Kahoe, after Mr. Kahoe," Mama B tells Papa Doc.
   "Done!" says Papa Doc.

A loud crow is heard from the chicken
house. Rufus seems to be celebrating the arrival
of the new animals on Bluebird Hill. Rufus' crow
reminds Mama B, who has been so busy with
other things, she has forgotten to feed the
chickens. She puts on the outside shoes she
wears to the chicken house and her bonnet.
Hurriedly she goes to the chicken house, to feed
her little flock of chickens. Cream and all her
little biddies that hatched in the spring, greet
Mama B at the chicken yard gate.
   All the chickens gather around and make
their usual chicken sounds as Mama B chats
with them using human words. After feeding
the chickens and having a nice visit, she gathers

the eggs and gently places them in her feed bucket.

When Kahoe, the young bull, is delivered to the farm the next day, he is decidedly not a happy bull. First of all, he was taken from his family and put in the back of a horrible, noisy, hot trailer. The big truck pulling the trailer took him to the animal clinic in Tylertown where Kahoe was given his inoculation shots. Once released into the Bluebird Hill pasture, an angry and upset Kahoe, desires nothing but solitude. He retreats to the farthest corner of the pasture and stays there.

"Mama B," says Papa Doc that evening. "Should we be concerned about Kahoe's behavior?"

"Not a bit. You mark my words, that handsome creature will be just fine tomorrow. We just have to give him time to get over the rough day he had today," says Mama B.

Sure enough, the next day, Kahoe seems to have forgotten all about his other family of cows as well as his shots. He is a happy bull and fits right in on Bluebird Hill with Mama Cow, Paprika, Mower and Midnight.

Kahoe is a good companion for the cows and is even friendly to humans. But Mama B never takes a chance with him because bulls can be dangerous. She always stays outside of the fence from Kahoe when he eats from her hand. He is such fun as he licks sweet feed or corn from her hand with his big rough black tongue. Then

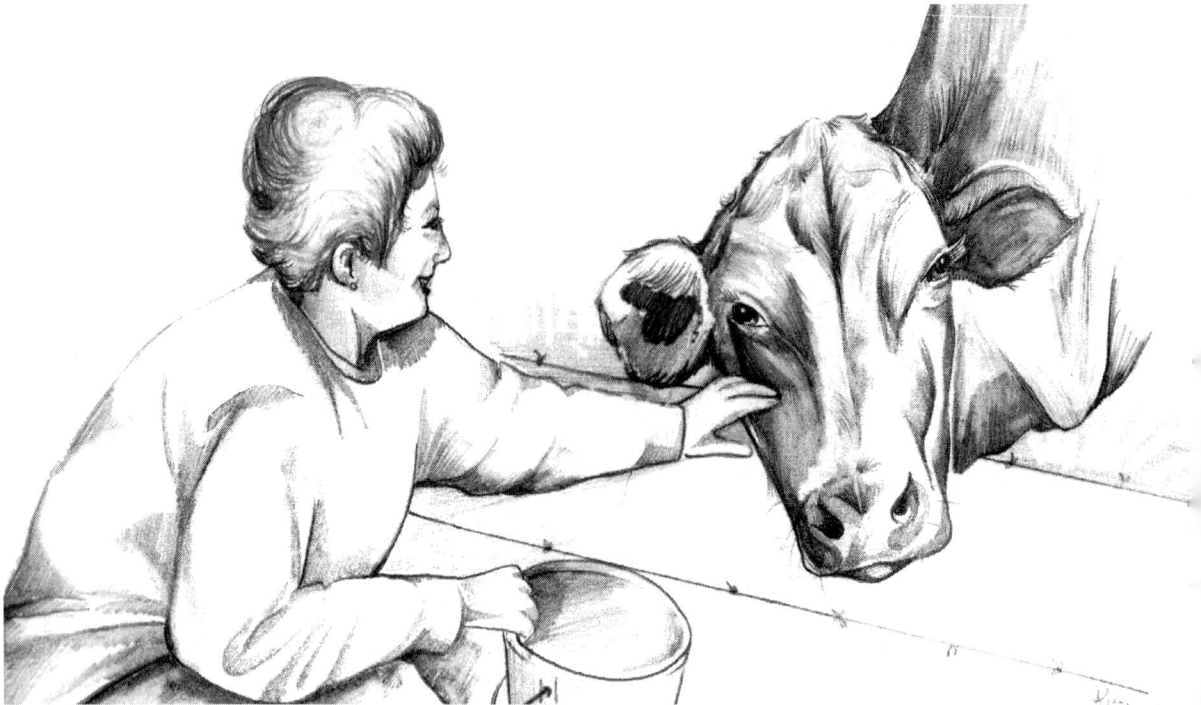

when he's finished he stands still so she can scratch him between the eyes. He moves his big head up and down as Mama B's hand follows the movement of his head. It looks as if he is saying, *yes, yes, scratch more, scratch more.*

Kahoe likes to entertain himself by rubbing or pushing anything he can move with his head. His favorite thing to do is to push Papa Doc's flat boat into the pond. Papa Doc gets very upset with Kahoe. He has to get his pirogue, which is a smaller boat that looks like a canoe, in order to rescue the flat boat that Kahoe has pushed into the water.

Mama B tells Papa Doc to get ready to enlarge the pasture. "In a couple of years," she says, "we will be increasing our herd of cows with baby Kahoes, as Midnight and Paprika become mamas."

"Maybe Kahoe will be so busy with his little ones that he will leave my flat boat alone," says Papa Doc.

Papa Doc looks at Mama B with his brown

beaded eyes and says, "Let's go get an ice cold slice of watermelon and sit on the porch to eat it. We now have time to sit because, as you promised, the cows are eating the grass that we used to mow."

Just as they have their first bites of watermelon they both notice their little friend Fritz, the unusual squirrel with the unusual name, peeking from behind a ball of mistletoe that is growing in the big oak tree. Suddenly he jumps out as if he is trying to scare Mama B and Papa Doc. Bo, who has been laying on the porch by Mama B's feet, sees Fritz and runs to the base of the big oak tree. *Bark! Bark! Bark!*

Fritz teases Bo by coming down the tree head first just close enough to make Bo think he's going to get him. But quick as a wink, Fritz turns around and starts back up the tree, he stops, makes a few sounds and flicks his tail at Bo.

Bark! Bark! Bark! an insulted Bo answers. But it's really too hot to be angry and Bo comes back to the shade of the porch where he licks a few drops of sweet watermelon juice that have dropped on the porch floor.

Kahoe, Mama Cow, Paprika, Mower, and Midnight, are standing at the pasture fence watching Mama B and Papa Doc on the porch. The cows and Kahoe are chewing their cud. A cud is the once-swallowed food they are chewing again. They chew their cud using their back teeth just enough to swallow it. Cattle have a

stomach with four compartments. This allows them to bring the food back from their stomach and chew and swallow the food again. They chew their food two separate times to digest it. It looks like they are chewing bubble gum as they stand and chew and swish their tails.

Papa Doc is watching the cows and thinking about how useful these animals are to everyone. "We drink their milk and use it to make butter, ice cream and cheese. You know, Mama B, I just don't think I could survive without my milk and cookies," says Papa Doc with a little grin.

Mama B smiles, she knows he is right. He has to have his cookies and a cup of milk every night at bedtime or he gets grumpy.

It is the end of August. The temperature is usually ninety degrees or more during the day in southern Mississippi.

"Papa Doc," Mama B says, "shall we plan a trip down to the beach at Gulfport? Or how about we drive the circle and do some shopping in Hattiesburg?"

Now Papa Doc, who is not one who ever enjoys shopping, looks at Mama B with his little brown beaded eyes and she knows that he won't be doing any shopping. But when she mentions visiting some of Hattiesburg's wonderful restaurants, a twinkle comes into his eyes and he nods slowly in agreement. Papa Doc is looking forward to a little trip but most of all, he is happy to have the leisure to enjoy sitting on the porch. He truly appreciates the beauty of the summer and the pleasant company of their cows.

The summer showers are slacking off now. The hay is being cut and bailed for the cows to eat in the autumn and winter. The grass is not growing as fast, and with the arrival of autumn, the grass will stop growing; except for the planted winter grass. It's a great day, On Bluebird Hill. The cool days of autumn are on the way.

The End (for now)

RECIPE

From Mama B's farm kitchen

HAY STACKS

1 (6 oz.) Package Butterscotch Morsels
2 Teaspoons Salad Oil
1 (3 oz.) Can Chow Mein Chinese
Noodles
1 Small Can Salted Peanuts

In a heavy boiler over low heat (or follow directions on package), melt butterscotch morsels. Stir in salad oil. In a large bowl, mix chow mein noodles and peanuts. Pour on melted butterscotch and mix thoroughly with a fork. Drop mixture by teaspoonfuls on waxed paper or greased cookie sheet. Cool and enjoy!